THE ANTICHRIST OF REVELATION

666

ERIKA GREY

Copyright © 2013 Erika Grey

All rights reserved.

Library of Congress Control Number: 2013949091

ISBN:978-0-9790199-6-8
ISBN-13:0-9790199-6-6

DEDICATION

To my children

For Books and Articles
by Erika Grey go to
www.erikagrey.com

CONTENTS

	Introduction	vii
1	The Antichrist	1
2	The Antichrist and Jesus: Biblical Contrasts	15
3	The Antichrist Rises From the Tribe of Dan	23
4	The Person of the Antichrist	31
5	The Antichrist and His Mark	39
6	The Abomination of Desolation	47
7	Antichrist's: 200 Million	61
8	Ten Days of Tribulation	67
9	God's Judgments	75
10	Warning and Promise	85

INTRODUCTION

It was not long after I became a Christian that I heard of the Antichrist. His very name evokes fear. He is the embodiment of all evil. He is also the son of Satan who will walk this Earth and be given the power to rule it. He will unleash his fury on those who do not worship him as god.

Unlike dictators before him, he possesses superior intellect and his government will have world rule. Yet, he shares many of the same traits of evil leaders before him, and they provide a glimpse into the horrors of life under his regime. The Antichrist is Jesus Christ's nemesis, and he takes a role in the battle of the ages between God and Satan. It is God who allows his reign for His divine purposes.

Through the years, Christians have asked many questions about the Antichrist, and a variety of myths have surfaced. This book answers those inquiries and corrects the myths. In addition, I reveal a good deal of information that is not common knowledge but is in the Bible concerning the person of the Antichrist.

I have met several self-righteous souls who feel that we should not spend time talking about the Antichrist. He is in the Bible, and he is there for a reason. He will be involved in a significant time in Israel's and the world's history. He ushers in the end of the world. To worship him equals spiritual death, but to defy him equals physical death and eternal life. For us today he is our warning of what is to come, and if you do not know Jesus Christ as your personal savior, you need to be afraid. If you are a Christian, you must be diligent and watching as Christ commanded and ready for when the King returns.

ERIKA GREY

1
THE ANTICHRIST

Nearly all evangelical Christians have learned of the Antichrist. He horrifies, mystifies and fills us with dread. He is the world dictator who the Bible forecasts arrives into his position during the Earth's final years.

Every generation of Christians has talked about him. Even the apostles questioned Jesus about the Antichrist, and they mentioned him in their books. Jesus's teachings on him also mystified the church fathers Irenaeus (A.D. 120-202) and his disciple Hippolytus A.D. 170-236 who was a hearer of Polycarp and a disciple of John. They discussed the Antichrist in detail, which reveals the early church members preoccupation with the end of the world and the Antichrist.

We become so fixated on the Antichrist we forget he is only a part of the judgments that will be unleashed on the Earth before the destruction of the world and during the Tribulation. Never-the-less, the Antichrist's dictatorship provides the atmosphere of life in the world's final seven years called by Jesus in Matthew and Revelation the Tribulation.

7 Years of Tribulation

The Tribulation is a seven-year period of wars, plagues, famines, earthquakes, and natural disasters. It ushers in the government of the Antichrist and his final world empire. It ends in the Battle of Armageddon, and the Second Coming of Jesus Christ. The Antichrist's dictatorship reigns supreme during this time of God's wrath. Part of the Earth's judgments happen through the Antichrist.

The book of Daniel specifically defines the time period as a week, which is a seven-year period of time. Daniel details the abomination of desolation, which occurs in the middle of the week, and Jesus tells us that after this event will be great tribulation. Daniel actually provides the number of days from the middle of the Tribulation to the end.

Peace Treaty With Israel

All Bible prophecy centers around the nation of Israel. The Tribulation begins when the Antichrist signs a peace treaty with

Israel guaranteeing Israel peace. The Antichrist is a deceiver, and he deceives Israel into believing he is the nation's ally.

In several places in Scripture, the Bible elaborates on the deceit behind this agreement. God tells Israel they have made lies their refuge. In the book of Isaiah, God reveals the truth of this covenant. Isaiah 28:15, 18 reads:

Because you have said, We have made a covenant with death, and with Sheol, we are in agreement: when the overflowing scourge passes through, it will not come to us; for we have made lies our refuge, and under falsehood, we have hidden ourselves.

Your covenant with death will be annulled, and your agreement with Sheol will not stand; when the overflowing scourge passes through, then you will be trampled down by it.

God is telling the Jewish nation that "*with hell they are in agreement*" because the man they are dealing with is none other than the Devil in a man's body. The phrase "*we have made lies our refuge*" exposes that the guarantees of the treaty are false. The Antichrist hates Israel and has no intention of helping the nation rather he will seek to destroy it. God tells them that "*when the overflowing scourge passes through, you will be trampled down by it.*" Other words, when the Antichrist wages war against Israel, the nation will be annihilated by it. God elaborates on the Antichrist's deception and intention as he signed this agreement. In Psalm 55: 20-21 it says:

He has put forth his hands against those who were at peace with him:
He has broken his covenant.
The words of his mouth were smoother than butter,
But war was in his heart;
His words were softer than oil,
Yet they were drawn swords.

Scripture provides a view to the emotional and physical picture of Israel once the Antichrist breaks the treaty and lays siege to the nation. Isaiah 33:7-9 states:

Surely, their valiant ones shall cry outside: the ambassadors of peace shall weep bitterly.
The highways lie waste; the wayfaring man ceases.
He has broken the covenant; he despised the cities; he regards no man. The Earth mourns and languishes; Lebanon is ashamed and shriveled: Sharon is like a wilderness: and Bashan and Carmel shake off their fruits.

These passages mentioned Israel being at peace with him and the weeping of the ambassadors of peace. These verses clarify that the covenant is an agreement for peace. What should be noted is the phrase "covenant of death." In the Revelation Death and Hades are thrown into the lake of fire (Rev. 20:14). We see Death again as the rider of the fourth horse of the Revelation and Hades follows him. (Rev. 6:8). It is my interpretation that Death and Hades are the principalities, and powers talked about in Ephesians 6:12:

For we do not wrestle against flesh and blood, but against principalities, against powers, against the rulers of the darkness of this age, against spiritual hosts of wickedness in the heavenly places.

Death and Hades are rulers of darkness that are directly beneath Satan. The "Covenant with Death" and "Agreement with Hell" is with these two principalities and powers who are underneath Satan. When the Antichrist signs this treaty, he knows what he is going to do to Israel. The Antichrist becomes the henchman of his father the Devil to cause death and damn souls to hell. Thus, we see the triage of the Antichrist, Death and Hades.

The Antichrist Regards No Man

The Antichrist will also cause tremendous hardship and suffering on those he wages war against. The Isaiah passage tells us he "regards no man."' This means he does not have any compassion or empathy for anyone in the human race. He is worse than a sociopath or psychopath. Daniel 11:37 elaborates on the Antichrist's regard for no man. It states: *"He shall regard neither the God of his fathers, nor the desire of women, nor regard any god: for he shall magnify himself above them all."* Genesis 3:16 teaches that Eve represented all of womanhood. Her *"desire shall be for your husband."* The desire of women is man. Thus, the Antichrist will regard no man.

The Scriptures detail the Antichrist's reign of terror. Due to his anti-God, anti-Christ policies, Evangelical circles customarily refer to him as the Antichrist. The Bible mentions this title only once in the Scriptures (1John 2:18). The Devil enters this man's body and wreaks havoc on the world. His reign ignites the Battle of Armageddon (Is. 14:12; Ezek. 28:3-4).

Names of the Antichrist

Evidencing the Antichrist's significance, over thirty titles relate to him in both the Old and New Testaments. These include:

The Bloody and Deceitful Man Ps. 5-6
Wicked One Ps. 10:2-4

The Man of the Earth Ps. 10:18
The Mighty Man Ps. 52:1
The Enemy Ps. 53:3
The Adversary Ps. 74:8-10
The Head of Many Countries Ps. 111:6
The Violent Man Ps. 140:1
The Assyrian Is. 10:5-12
The King of Babylon Is. 14:2
The Sun of the Morning Is. 14:12
The Spoiler Is. 16:4-5; Jer. 6:26
The Nail Is. 22:25
The Branch of the Terrible Ones Is. 25:5
The Profane Wicked Prince of Israel Ezek. 21:25-27
The Little Horn Dan. 7:8
The Prince That Shall Come Dan. 9:26
The Vile Person Dan. 11:121
The Willful King Dan. 11:36
The Idol Shepherd Zech. 11:16-17
The Man of Sin 2 Thess. 2:3
The Son of Perdition 2 Thess. 2:3
The Lawless One 2 Thess. 2:8
The Angel of the Bottomless Pit Rev. 9:1
Another Coming in His Own Name John 5:43
The King of Fierce Countenance Dan. 8:23
The Abomination of Desolation Matt. 24:15
The Desolator Dan. 9:27
The King of Tyre Ezek. 28:12
The Lion Jer. 4:6-7
The destroyer of the nations Jer. 4:6-7
Lucifer Is. 14:12

1 John 2:18, identifies him as the Antichrist, a liar who denies the Father and the Son. Rev. 13:1 refers to him as "the Beast," and later in the passage names him 666. The number six, translated from the New Testament Greek into English, means "vex," or "curse." Seven represents God's number of perfection. The triple six represents the unholy trinity, with the Devil acting as God. The Antichrist, whom Satanists call the son of Satan, mimics Jesus Christ. The False Prophet who the Bible predicts will come to the Earth and performs miracles to get the masses to worship the Beast, mocks God's Holy Spirit. The unholy trinity are named in Scriptures as "The Dragon," "The Beast," and "The False Prophet."

Unlike previous dictators, Satan, himself possesses the Antichrist. He obtains the world's respect by bringing the world prosperity, until the day he declares himself a god and demands worship for himself alone. Once the Antichrist establishes himself as a deity his evil side manifests itself.

Seat of Antichrist

Revelation 13:2 tells us that Satan provides the Antichrist with a *"great seat of authority,"* i.e., the political position he will hold. The Antichrist's "great *seat of authority*" becomes the highest position of the most powerful government to exist. Despite its earthly might, it does not compare to the heavenly kingdom of Jesus Christ.

The Antichrist's reign on Earth will completely contrast our Lord's. Unlike Christ, whom the masses rejected, the Antichrist they will accept. In John 5:43, Christ affirms: *"I have come in My Father's name, and you do not receive Me; if another comes in his own name, him you will receive."* This verse also happens to be the one place here Jesus makes a direct reference to the Antichrist. Jesus came to save; Antichrist comes to destroy. Daniel refers to the Antichrist as a *"prince,"* with a lower-case p, while capitalizing the Prince of Peace.

Appointed by God

As surprising as this sounds, and as much as Christians speak out against the Antichrist and his coming world empire, he is appointed by God. Daniel said to Nebuchadnezzar King of Babylon in Daniel 2:38:

You O King, are a king of kings. For the God of heaven has given you a kingdom, power, strength and glory: And wherever the children of men dwell, or the beasts of the field and the birds of heaven. He has given them into your hand, and has made you ruler over them all—you are this head of gold.

The prophet Jeremiah spoke against the Babylonian empire and the coming king of Babylon who was a type of Antichrist. During his ministry, he preached against this future invasion and warned the Israelites of the coming judgment for their sin.

In return for his speaking God's word and warning them, the princes sent Jeremiah to a dungeon, which was basically a slushy dry well. They lowered Jeremiah into the mud and mire with ropes and left him to die of hunger. King Zedekiah had him pulled out to inquire of Jeremiah what he should do in the face of the invading Babylonians and Jeremiah told him he must surrender. However, instead of submitting he tried to flee and was captured and killed. He left Jeremiah in prison. Surprisingly Jeremiah ended up being protected by the King of Babylon, who took him out of prison. God used the evil king to shelter Jeremiah and judge the sinning Israelites in Jeremiah 39:17.

Then they sent someone to take Jeremiah from the court of the prison, and committed him to Gedaliah, the son of Ahikam, the son of Shapan, that he should take him home. So he dwelt among the people.

This did not mean that Jeremiah was not afraid of the Chaldeans because he was but God told him, *"For I will surely deliver you, and you shall not fall by the sword, but your life shall be as a prize to you, because you have put your trust in me."* So not only was the King of Babylon appointed by God to judge Israel, but God used him to protect Jeremiah.

This same king, Daniel served in his court and interpreted his dreams. Nebuchadnezzar liked Daniel and Daniel never judged him, but spoke God's word. Daniel understood that he was given his position by God. Likewise, the Antichrist is given his authority by God. We are told in Daniel 11:36, *...and (he) shall prosper till the wrath has been accomplished; for what has been determined shall be done.*

Revelation tells us in three places of the power given to him by God. Revelation 13:5, *..and he was given authority to continue for forty-two months.* Verse 7 states, *It was granted to him to make war with the saints and to overcome them. And authority was given him over every tribe, tongue and nation.* During the Tribulation God allows the Antichrist to make war with Christians and kill them. God also gives him dominion over all people on earth. We see in Revelation 6:10, the martyrs crying for vengeance under the alter towards those who took their lives.

The Antichrist's position is given by God, it is Satan who gives him his power, his throne, and great authority (Rev. 13:2).While Satan gives the Antichrist his government, it is God who gives him his rule, thus he is appointed by God. Satan has authority over all the kingdoms and governments of this world. Luke 4:5-7 confirms during the temptation of Jesus by the Devil:

Then the devil said to Him, All this authority I will give You and their glory; for this has been delivered to me, and I give it to whomever I wish, Therefore, if You will worship before me, all will be yours.

I am reminded of Elisha, who wept as he told Hazael that he would be king of Syria and the evil he would do against the children of Israel. 2 Kings 8:12 states:

And Hazael said, Why is my lord weeping? He answered, Because I know the evil that you will do to the children of Israel. Their strongholds you will set on fire, and their young men you will kill with the sword; and you will dash their children, and rip open their women with child.

Just as Hazael was part of God's purpose, so is the Antichrist in God's plan. Thus, he is appointed by God, meaning he will take his part in fulfill God's purpose. Jesus handpicked Judas Iscariot knowing full well he was a devil and told him, "*do what you must do*" in his betrayal against Jesus. Judas was part of God's purpose.

What does this mean It? means that when the Antichrist arrives, he is part of God's plan. Do we try to put a stop to him, no, do we speak out against his Kingdom? No we sit and observe. The action we must take is to make sure we know Jesus as our personal savior. If we know Him, we need to make sure that we are living our lives for Him and not letting a minute go to waste because there is not much time left. We are that close now to the end.

2

THE ANTICHRIST AND JESUS BIBLICAL CONTRASTS

Throughout the Bible are numerous contrasts of Jesus and the Antichrist. The many comparisons reveal the significance of the spiritual battle which began when God first cast Satan out of heaven. The Biblical definition of Satan means adversary. The Greek defines Devil as a false accuser. The Antichrist is our Lord Jesus Christ's evil counterpart and true rival.

The Unholy Trinity

Jesus is the son of God, and the Antichrist is the Son of Satan. Both function within a trinity. Jesus is part of the holy trinity (Father, Son and Holy Spirit) and the Antichrist belongs to the unholy trinity (Satan, Antichrist, and the False Prophet as the unholy spirit). Jesus' kingdom is in heaven, the Antichrist is here on Earth. The parallels are numerous. God sits upon a throne, and so does Satan (Rev. 2:13).

The Pride Lion vs. The Scavenger Lion

The Bible refers to Jesus as the Lion of the Tribe of Judah and calls Satan the roaring lion seeking who he will devour. The Antichrist is compared to a lion, which charges from the thicket. Jesus is the pride lion, which is the strongest male in a group of males and females. The pride males get this position because they has defeated all other male lions in battle to win the females.

The Bible compares Jesus to the regal, powerful male who leads the pride. The males who get old or who are too young or weak who get kicked out of the pride end up becoming scavengers. These males will wander without the protection of other lions and will sometimes team up with other nomads. Satan is compared to the scavenger lion which in nature is too weak to win against a pride male and is an outcast from the pride left to scavenge for food.

The Beast of Revelation, which is the Antichrist has the mouth of a lion (Rev. 13:2). and Daniel elaborates that the teeth are of iron (Daniel 7:19). Joel 1:6 also depicts the Antichrist as a lion in the prediction of the Antichrist's conquest of Israel, it states, *"For a nation has come up against My land, Strong, and without number; His teeth are the teeth of a lion, And he has the fangs of a fierce lion.*

The lion parallels of Jesus and the Antichrist are very evident in Scripture

Both Ride White Horses

While the Revelation depicts Jesus riding a white horse as the King of Kings, the Antichrist also steers a white horse, but he arrives as a prince of deception and a destroyer of life. Jesus brings life while the Antichrist brings death. The horseman of Revelation carries a bow, while Jesus brings a sword (Rev.6:2) The bow is a distance weapon, while the sword is for up close front line battle. A bow is also a hunting tool. This fits the Antichrist who will be searching for Christian and religious targets and he will like an archer who kills them with precision. In ancient wars the sword is the symbol of the warrior, the ultimate battle tool, while the bow typified the assassins who fought from the rear.

The masses see Jesus high up in the sky while the Antichrist is viewed lying on the ground at the end of the Battle of Armageddon. Jesus's horse rides in the heavens and the Antichrist's gallops on the earth. Jesus said My kingdom is not of this world because He reigns from the heavens while the Antichrist dominates the earth.

The Tree, Gospel, Mark and Numerology

Both came to this earth once before and hung on a tree. God said, "cursed is everyone that hangs on a tree"(Gal. 3:13, Deut.21:22-

23.) Jesus died on the cross and bore the curse of sin to release man from the curse so that all who place their faith and trust in trust in him for their salvation will have eternal life. Judas Iscariot who Jesus referred to as the son of perdition willingly hung himself on a tree as if marking Satan the curse for mankind so that all who believe his lies will live in eternal damnation. There is a teaching that teaches that Judas Iscariot who Jesus referred to as the Son of Perdition was the Antichrist and returns in the latter days. Satan directly entered into Judas, and scholars have concluded that Satan also goes into is the Antichrist.

Jesus came and the masses rejected Him. The Antichrist will come in his own name and the masses will accept him. Both come teaching a Gospel; Jesus preaches His Gospel while the Antichrist teaches of his strange god of forces and will deify himself. Both mark and seal their believers with God placing his seal on the redeemed and Satan through the Antichrist institutes the Mark of the Beast. Both kingdoms use numerology. Biblical (7, 40, 12, 3,) Antichrist (13, 666, 9, 6,) to name a few. In Jesus' letter to the seven churches, Satan, (also the devil) cited as a direct opponent of Jesus Christ, is referred to 6 times. Jesus teaches truth, while Satan relies on all false teachings. Jesus heals individuals; Antichrist comes to destroy them.

More Parallels

The Bible refers to Jesus as the chief cornerstone uniting his church; the Antichrist's government acts as the cornerstone for uniting the world. Jesus is the name above all names. The Antichrist has a number for his name. So throughout Scripture we find all the parallels, which reveal the significance of the Battle of the Ages.

Both Jesus and the Antichrist are Jews. Jesus is from the tribe of Judah, and the Antichrist will descend from the tribe of Dan, which became an outcaste tribe due to its practice of idolatry and was replaced by one of the son's of Joseph, in essence, Dan became the 13th tribe. We discuss this in the next chapter. We see this repeated again with the 12 apostles. Judas, also a Jew, who Jesus called the son of perdition was the outcast due to his idolatry and treason and replaced by another apostle—rendering Judas the 13th apostle with 13 a number of the Devil.

No doubt the Antichrist is alive today, and the parallels continue. Jesus was born from a virgin, a humble birth; one can only imagine the birth of the Antichrist. Jesus' parents were righteous, God-fearing Jews; the Antichrist's parents will no doubt be unrighteous, which can span the gamut of possibilities from their being incestuous to an occultist.

We see the Antichrist rising out of the sea with 10 horns upon his head, which are ten earthly kingdoms, and likewise, we see Jesus depicted with seven horns. "...in the midst of the elders, stood a Lamb as though it had been slain, having seven horns and seven eyes, which are the seven Spirits of God sent out into tall the earth. Rev. 5:6, now these seven horns represent the seven churches that Jesus Christ is King over. The Antichrist presides over an earthly kingdom and Jesus over the heavenly.

Jesus rose from the dead, and the Antichrist receives a wound unto death, and himself comes back from the dead. Revelation 13:3, 12. Jesus is God's son, and Satan was God's highest creation who tried to usurp the place of His Son in this world. In the temptation of Christ, Satan tried to approach him and take the place of the Father by telling Jesus he would give him the kingdoms of this world if He would worship Satan.

Just as Jesus's entire life was devoted to His ministry, the Antichrist as the son of Satan will be schooled in politics, finance and groomed to lead this world.

Satan, God's adversary has his own synagogue and throne and has battled against God and his people through the ages. Based on the prophetic time line and the predicted events which have come to pass, the Antichrist most likely was born and is now a man and quite possibly already a statesman poised to step into the political seat given to him by Satan: the seat of the Antichrist, and ready to take his role in the Battle of the Ages.

3

THE ANTICHRIST RISES FROM THE TRIBE OF DAN

Many wonder where the Antichrist will come from. What country will he be born in? They speculate on his nationality. Some ask will he will be Greek? Roman? Recent scholars are teaching that he will rise from an Islamic nation.

The Bible is very clear that the Antichrist will be Jewish and will have Jewish ancestry because he will come from the tribe of Dan. He might not look obviously Jewish and if his father is a Gentile, he might appear to be of another nationality.

In traditional Judaism, Jewish lineage comes from the mother not the father. They base this on several passages in the Torah such as Lev.24:10, which speaks of an Israelite woman and her Egyptian husband who "went out among the children of Israel" and their son was judged for his sin against the God of Israel. In Ezra 10:2-3 the men returning to Israel vowed to put away their

Jewish wives and the children born to them. These children were not considered among the children of Israel being born of pagan women, although their fathers were Jewish. So if the Antichrist has a Jewish mother but a Gentile father, he is Jewish.

The Antichrist will most likely come from a European country: western, central or east European. He will be Jewish and will either have a Jewish name, or a Gentile name if his father is a non-Jew.

Rachel's Sin of Idolatry

We know the Antichrist comes from the tribe of Dan, but Why Dan? To understand why we must look at Dan's origin. Rachel, the wife of Jacob was both beautiful and like most Biblical patriarchs had her area of sin. Rachel could not have any children and became jealous of her sister Leah, who bore Jacob 4 sons while she sat without children. She became angry at Jacob and blamed him for her childless state. In Rachel's jealousy, she grabbed her maid Bilhah, and gave her to Jacob as a surrogate to have children for her, and Bilhah bore Dan. Jealous rivalry continued between Rachel and Leah. Rachel's maid bore a second son to her: Naphtali.

When Jacob left the home of his father in law, Rachel stole his idols and lied to her father as he searched for them so that he would not find them. She also kept this secret from her husband Jacob, who did not know that she had robbed the idols from her dad. Rachel's attachment to the idols was so great that she stole them and lied to protect them. Rachel's sin was idolatry.

No doubt she was thrilled over the birth of Dan from her maid and doted over him, and he followed in her in the area of her idolatry.

Micah's Idol

Judges Chapters 17 and 18 tells the story of Micah an idolater who lived in the mountains of Ephraim and who employed a renegade, idolatrous priest. **The Tribe of Dan failed to conquer the portion of the land of Israel that was given to them as their original inheritance** Dan and 600 of his men went searching the land for an area to settle in and came upon Micah's house.. They forcibly took his idols and his priest to serve them. They then went into Laish whose people lived quietly and peacefully and took the land by murdering its inhabitants. They renamed it Dan and setup Micah's god and employed idolatrous priests to serve them until their captivity.

Dan murdered peaceful people and set up idolatry in defiance of Israel's God. In Scripture, currency is synonymous with idolatry. The image of Micah was constructed from money that the mother of a boy saved to make it into an idol, which ended up in

Micah's home. In my book The Empire: Bible Prophecy and the European Union, I write about the Mark of the Beast and point out other Biblical examples of currency turned into idols, these are all forerunners of the image and number of the Beast including Micah's idol.

Dan a Center for Idolatry

King Jeroboam, Israel's northern kingdom's first king who the Bible mentions repeatedly as "the man who caused Israel to sin" placed two golden calves, which he set up for idolatrous worship. He placed one in Bethel and the other in Dan which both lay on the extreme southern and northern part of the kingdom. (I Kings 29-30) Bethel afterwards became a center for Idolatry. Dan already existed as one, which is why Jeroboam placed a calf there. In Amos, which foretells Israel's captivity, in Amos God's references the idolatry of Dan for its allegiance to its false gods and declares judgment on idolaters. Amos 8:14 declares.

Those who swear by the sin of Samaria, Who say, As your god lives O Dan! And As the say of Beersheba lives! They shall fall and never rise again.

"The sin of Samaria" refers to a name, Ashima, a Canaanite mother-goddess. The way of Beersheba also relates to idolatry and the reference to *"as your god lives O Dan"* which confirms Dan's idolatrous god that they placed before the Lord God of Israel.

The Bible well establishes the idolatry of the tribe of Dan. This is one reason it is not mentioned among the 12 tribes in Revelation chapter 7 and is the lineage of the Antichrist. The Antichrist sets himself up as a god in the Jewish Temple and his beast as an idol, which he causes the False Prophet to worship and commits the ultimate idolatry and abomination.

Dan a Judge and Serpent

There is another reason Dan is not among the twelve tribes of Israel. Genesis 49:16 tells us that Dan shall judge his people as one of the tribes of Israel. The word used for judge means to act as a judge, minister judgment, requite, vindicate, govern, contend, strive, to be at strife, quarrel. Dan will judge his people meaning that the Antichrist will be from the tribe of Dan and will cause them the greatest hardship by acting as a judge for his people and be used in their recompense.

Genesis 49: 17 continues *"Dan shall be a serpent by the way and adder in the path that bites the horse's heels so that its rider shall fall backward."* When we think of the serpent, we think of the Devil who tempted Eve. Dan is a type of Devil whose idolatrous ways will influence the rest of the tribes in having them fall backwards into idolatry and its lies vs. their allegiance to the God of Israel. This is Satan's work in Israel and through the ages among the Gentiles.

Jeremiah 8:16 which prophesies about the last days' states:

The snorting of his horses was heard from Dan. The whole land trembled at the sound of the neighing of hits strong ones: For they have come and devoured the land and all that is in it. The city and those who dwell in it.

In the same context 17 continues "*For behold I will send serpents among you, Vipers, which cannot be charmed. And they shall bite you, says the Lord.* This verse elaborates on the prediction that Dan will judge his people. His being a serpent, by the way, and is talking about the Antichrist's siege of Israel during the Tribulation. These vipers cannot be charmed because they have one intent in mind, and that is to destroy the Jews. *"The whole land trembles at the neighing of his strong ones"* refers to the Antichrist's army. In the previous, chapter I spoke about the many Biblical contrasts of Jesus and the Antichrist. Jesus rises from the Tribe of Judah and the Antichrist from the Tribe of Dan.

Both Tribes as Lion

Both Jesus and the Antichrist are symbolized by lions, with Jesus being the pride lion and the Antichrist the scavenger Lion. Both Jesus and Dan are referred to as a Lion's whelp in Scripture and this parallel is also found in Genesis 49:9 (Judah) and Deuteronomy 33:22. (Dan) Moses stated of Dan in the verse, *"Dan is lion's whelp; He shall leap from Bashan."* Likewise Jacob in Genesis 49:9, *"Judah is a lion's whelp."* In an earlier chapter I discussed the Antichrist depicted as having the mouth of a lion.

In conclusion both Jesus and the Antichrist are Jews and while the Messiah comes from the tribe of Judah, the False Messiah arrives from the tribe of Dan Jesus said that He came in his father's name and was not received but one coming in his own name will be received (John 5: 43). Jesus was speaking to the Jews here and referring to Himself and the Antichrist who like Jesus will rise from Jewish lineage The Bible is very clear about the Antichrist's origins.

Finally, another verse that sites the Antichrist's origins is found in Daniel 11:37, describing the Antichrist it states, *"He shall neither regard the God of his fathers.* The fathers refer to Abraham, Isaac and Jacob, who are the fathers of the nation of Israel and believed in God. "Thus the Antichrist will be Jewish, and he will trace to the tribe of Dan.

4

THE PERSON OF THE ANTICHRIST

The mysterious frightening language of the Revelation leaves us mystified and terrified and curious, especially when it comes to the person of the Antichrist. Who is he, what will he look like? Myths have surfaced and anyone who embraces these legends is not paying attention to what the Scriptures teach about him. Some teachers have depicted the Antichrist as a handsome man with perfect features smiling from ear to ear, deceiving the world by his charismatic charm and good looks. This is not the portrayal of the Antichrist in the Bible. Nowhere in the Bible does it tell us he is good looking or captivating

Rude, Bold, Arrogant

What the Bible tells us about the appearance of the Antichrist is this: Daniel 8: 23 states, *"And in the latter time of their kingdom, When the transgressors have reached their fullness, A king shall arise,*

Having fierce features." The word means strong, mighty, fierce. The word in Daniel 8:23 specifically means hard of face shameless, not showing respect for another person, rude. Synonyms are insolent meaning the person is marked by contemptuous or cocky boldness or disregard of others. They are impolite , highly insulting, condescending in speech or conduct, overbearing. We also get from these words exhibiting boldness.

Daniel 7:20 tells us that the Antichrist's appearance is greater than his fellows and the word used in the Hebrew means chief, captain, leader, it also means pronounced, to speak great things, to talk proudly, impiously, which relates to his establishing himself as a deity.

Many believe the Antichrist is going to be charismatic, so charming the world will want to flock to him. Nowhere in Scripture does it say the Antichrist is charismatic and a charmer, if anything he will stand out as a leader and one who is cocky and bold. The Bible focuses more on his words which are blasphemous than his looks. The Antichrist does not get into his position by his charm. The Scripture tells us that he obtains the kingdom through intrigue- a secret or underhand scheme; a plot.

In earlier chapters I spoke of the contrasts of Jesus and the Antichrist. Jesus was marked by humility, kindness, and love. His personality is the opposite of the Antichrists who is proud, cocky and arrogant.

Brilliant, Real Smart, Wiser Than Daniel

The Scripture tells us that the Antichrist is smarter than Daniel, One thing we know about his person is that he is brilliant. Ezekiel 28:3-5 deems him *"wiser than Daniel"* for *"there is no secret"* hidden from him. The Antichrist's genius is greater than Daniel's, whose intelligence surpassed that of all the other prophets and Old Testament patriarchs. Daniel was skillful in all learning, knowledge, and wisdom. He understood science and comprehended the most difficult concepts. Daniel also possessed the ability to interpret dreams and visions (Dan. 1:4,17, 5:11-12).

In addition to having wisdom like Solomon, he possessed the mind of a scholar, scientist, and mathematician. Recognized for his brilliant mind, Daniel served in Nebuchadnezzar's court as Master over all the wise men, the consultants to the king. When Darius the Median (the Medo-Persian Empire succeeded the Babylonian) took over Babylon, he appointed 120 princes to rule over the whole kingdom. Governing over the princes were three presidents, of whom Daniel was first. All the officials were accountable to him (Dan. 6:1-3). When Cyrus the Persian succeeded Darius, Daniel served and prospered during his reign as well. Daniel acted as the chief consultant to kings who ruled two of the four world empires that once existed.

Ezekiel confirms the Antichrist's intelligence stating by *"wisdom"* and *"understanding,"* he accumulates *"riches and gold and silver"* into his treasuries. Ezekiel concludes: *"By your great wisdom in trade you have increased your riches, and your heart is lifted up because of your riches."*

Isaiah 10:13 confirms the Antichrist's estimation of his wisdom. *"For he says, By the strength of my hand, I have done it, and by my wisdom, for I am prudent; Also I have removed the boundaries of the people, and have robbed their treasuries; So I have put down the inhabitants like a valiant man."*

The Antichrist will understand government, and finance and his abilities will enable him to rise to world leadership.

He Is Sinister, Cunning and Deceitful

Along with being smart, Daniel 8:23 tells us he will understand sinister schemes. He knows what he is doing and knows how to get into position. The King James Bible uses the phrase, "dark sentences," which is another definition for the word in the Hebrew that also means sinister schemes. This means he will comprehend difficult topics. He will know the solutions to the various problems within the EU, but he is really going to move the EU into its position of strength for his own purposes.

Most likely the Antichrist is at this moment already within the European Union acting like he is for the European Union's goals and for the European people. However, he sees his potential for total and absolute power within the EU. He does not care about Europe or the world, he cares about power. He will try to get into the EU's seat of power, which is the seat of authority given to him by Satan. Revelation 13:2 tells us that *"the dragon gave him his power, his throne and great authority."*

The Antichrist through his cunning will cause deceit to prosper under his rule. (Daniel 8:25). Politically speaking this means that he will tell the people one thing and do another. According to Daniel, the Antichrist is extremely skillful in this type of deception via his cabinet, intelligence agencies and army. We saw the same behavior with Adolph Hitler and his final solution to exterminate the Jews, which was to be kept secret from his own people and from the world.

He Becomes Strong With a Small People

Daniel tells us the Antichrist becomes strong with a small people (Daniel 11:23), which means it is a small country or electorate that puts him into power, but he raises his position to its greatness. Notice he does not get his great seat by the masses putting him there.

I believe the Antichrist is from a small country, and then he gets into the European Union and is elected by the groups within the EU council and Parliament to his position. Daniel also tells us that here is no pomp or circumstance when he gets into position. He is not given the honor of a king. This describes each European Union presidency, which are appointed and for which there is no pomp or circumstance.

It should be noted that the Antichrist slips into his position undetected by the masses. He becomes strong with a small people and there is no big ceremony when he gets into his position. Most likely he favors their cause and wins them. He raises this little horn position to the south, east and toward the Glorious Land (Daniel 8:9).

In the Revelation, the Antichrist comes on a white horse because he is a deceiver, and many will believe his words that he stands on the teachings of his ideology, that he is for Europe, human rights, and the good of the people. He is the opposite. Initially, when he sits in the EU's highest seat, he will continue to deceive to accomplish his aims, and he will. He does not gain his position because he is a great charmer or so charismatic but through intrigue and becoming strong with a small people. Satan is there to help him get into his position. In addition, the Antichrist is appointed by God for God's purpose and He gives him his world-wide authority.

Antichrist Rises From Dead

It should be noted that while the Antichrist is not charismatic, the False Prophet is. The Bible tells us about the False Prophet in Revelation 13: 12, *And he exercises all the authority of the first beast in his presence, and causes the Earth and those who dwell in it to worship the first beast, whose deadly wound was healed.* In regard to the Antichrist's wound Revelation 13 tells us, there is an eighth head on our seven headed beast who dies and comes back to life. Zachariah 11:17 elaborates on the wound and tells us his right eye is blinded, and his left arm dried up.

This injury can occur from an accident or from an assassination attempt. This wound further identifies him. He might end up wearing special glasses or an eye patch. His arm might be in some sort of a sling. Alternatively, he will not move it because of its paralysis. The Antichrist's injury and recovery from near death is in part how he will get the world's attention. This is also another parallel with Jesus.

The Antichrist is already walking, talking and living on Earth. He has just not stepped into his position yet. The European Union is the Final World Empire, and the Antichrist will hold a leading position within the EU. The Antichrist arrives in the right place at the most opportune time. His astute abilities in national and international finance help him to direct the EU into great prosperity. His genius leads them into superpower status.

After the Tribulation begins when the Antichrist makes the covenant of peace with Israel (Dan. 9:27 and his government agrees to act as the guarantor of the nation's peace, prosperity follows the first three and a half years after the agreement. The Antichrist raises the EU into a great economic and political world power. Nations flourish through trade and association with him. The Antichrist wins the favor with the masses because he leads the European Union into great wealth and all associated nations will prosper. He is smart, bold, outspoken and deceitful.

After he signs the treaty, which we spoke of earlier, which also elaborates on his deception. The Scripture tells us that while he speaks peace, his words are drawn swords, the four horsemen of Revelation are released. Men kill one another. Nation will fight against nation, and famines will plague the world. The Antichrist will use these wars to his advantage and despite the famines, he raises his empire to its zenith of power to enable it to become the fearsome, monstrous beast described in Daniel and the Revelation.

5

THE ANTICHRIST & HIS MARK

The Antichrist allies himself with "the False Prophet" (Rev. 19:20), a member of the unholy trinity. A renowned religious leader able to perform miracles he campaigns for the Antichrist. In this time frame, the Antichrist institutes the Mark of the Beast, worldwide. No person can buy or sell unless he wears it.

Taking the Mark of the Beast causes one to spend their eternity in hell. For those who do not know about the mark, it is mentioned twice in the Revelation and referenced to in six verses. It is the mark that the Antichrist will make everyone take and wear on their wrists or on their foreheads during his reign. According to the Revelation, no man will be able to buy or sell without the mark. Years ago, Evangelical Christians knew that this would be a high tech method of buying and selling, and it became big news when there came talk of a cash less society and credit and debit cards became the norm. In around the year 2000, emerged identification implants, called sub-dermal implants, (verichip, RFID chip) which marketed to pet owners to identify their lost pets and is also used for medical purposes and to track criminals. Of all names, the company is called Digital Angel. It was literally right out of the book of Revelation, and the Evangelical Christian community spread the news like a wild fire.

Mark Mimics Holy Spirit and Seal on Believers

In Revelation, we are told in several passages that anyone who takes the Mark of the Beast will go to hell. This mark is more than a payment system since it causes the bearer to lose their chance at heaven and damn them to hell. As a counterfeit to the kingdom of God the Antichrist seals those who are His via his mark. It is more than just a counterfeit, he mimics God and attempts to establish himself as God on Earth.

We get God's mark, by trusting in Jesus as our Savior, by making Him first in our life and by worshiping Him as savior. The Holy Spirit connects us with God. In the six verses about the mark, we read in the same verse that those who took the mark worshiped the image of the Beast. This worship and the taking of the mark go together.

The Antichrist will be connected to his followers just as Jesus is connected to His through the Holy Spirit. In my book, The Empire: Bible Prophecy and The European Union, I made mention of a quote from a scientist of what was next on the horizon. It is called brain interface, and it allows one to think a thought and cause an action in a computer. It has been used so far for medical reasons, such as with a robotic limb. A person can think a thought and cause it to move. At first, it required being hooked up to a helmet full of electrodes, but now it only requires an implantable device. There are also devices that do not have to be implanted and can rest on the outer brain.

Connecting One Brain to Another

The technology even connected two brains, a human and a rat. A man could wave the tail of a rat. In another study a scientist connected to his colleagues brains from across campus and caused him to move his mouse on his computer. According to Future Tense "It's like they're reading my mind, how next-generation apps will market your brainwaves.

In the last few years, the cost of EEG devices has dropped considerably, and consumer-grade headsets are becoming more affordable and can now be purchased for as little as $100. Companies are looking to these devices to produce games, self-monitoring tools, touch free keyboards and hands-free game controller

Future of Technology

Auto manufacturers are exploring BCIs to detect drivers' drowsiness levels and improve their reaction time. Market researchers want to use data from these same BCI devices to measure the attention level and emotional responses of focus groups to various advertisements and products.

Scientists are skeptical of the efficacy of these tools, but companies are nevertheless, rushing to bring them to consumers. Companies could detect whether you're paying attention to ads, how you feel about them, and whether they are personally relevant to you. Imagine an app that can detect when you're hungry and show you ads for restaurants or select music playlists according to your mood. Health insurance companies could use EEG data to determine your deductible based on EEG-recorded stress levels. Companies will be able to identify risk indicators for things like suicide, depression, or emotional instability.

Government Works Inc., is developing BCI headsets for lie detection and criminal investigations. By measuring a person's responses to questions and images, evidence collected from these devices has already been used in criminal trials. Although many question the reliability of these devices.

A company has also come out with a phone that you do not have to speak into; you wear a collar around your neck and think, and it picks up the vibrations and converts them to sound. According to the EU Commission and note that I quote the Commission because this is where the Mark will originate from, the revived Roman Empire, i.e. the European Union.

Computer scientists have predicted that within the next twenty years neural interfaces will be designed that will not only increase the dynamic range of senses, but will also enhance memory and enable "cyber think" — invisible communication with others.

Other Uses of Implantable Devices

Other potential uses of implantable ICT devices include using the human body as a medium for transmission of data (and energy) to "other devices" like PDAs (Personal Digital Assistant), cellular phones, medical devices (for surveillance purposes: like, for instance, in retired people's homes),

RFID is making possible to localize other persons. In a family website, your children could log into the surveillance system and look at what their parents or grandparents are doing.

Applied Digital Solutions (ADS), which created the VeriChip™, announced in April 2004 a partnership with gun manufactures to produce so-called "smart guns". Such weapons can be fired only if operated by their owner with a RFID-chip implanted in his or her hand.

Image of the Beast Clone of Antichrist

One of the passages that mention eternal damnation for taking the mark is Revelation 14:9-11 and it reads:

Then a third angel followed them, saying with a loud voice, "If anyone worships the beast and his image, and receives his mark on his forehead or on his hand,
he himself shall also drink of the wine of the wrath of God, which is poured out full strength into the cup of His indignation. He shall be tormented with fire and brimstone in the presence of the holy angels and in the presence of the Lamb.
And the smoke of their torment ascends forever and ever; and they have no rest day or night, who worship the beast and his image, and whoever receives the mark of his name.

Based on the technology available today, the image of the beast will be some sort of a computerized clone of the Antichrist. He will have access to every single person via his mark, and the computer will provide him the ultimate control over his police state and over the population. To take the mark you will directly hook to the Antichrist and give your soul and mind to him. The Antichrist's computer clone, the False Prophet will give the breath of life to and make to speak. People will be amazed and will literally worship this scientific stride.

Antichrist Honors God of Technology

Daniel 11:17-18 tells us the Antichrist will not honor any god for he exalts himself above all, but in their place, he shall honor a god of fortresses, and a god which his fathers did know he shall honor, the King James says it this way, *Thus shall he do in the most strong holds with a strange god, whom he shall acknowledge and increase with glory: and he shall cause them to rule over many, and shall divide the land for gain..*
This strange, foreign god that his fathers did not know is the god of the technology for his police state, which connects him to his people and numbers 666. This mind, people controlling, computer mainframe that looks like him, he places in the holy of holies as its home as if to say he is God.

The Mark Equals Damnation

To take the mark will mean that you will be directed and controlled by the Antichrist or his government. They will know your every move and thought. Worse, he will be able to put their thoughts into your mind. Just like the Holy Spirit speaks to us about spiritual truths.

To accept the mark you give all of yourself to the Antichrist and his government. In giving yourself over to him and his government, i.e. the Beast, you worship him. He will seek out those who do not take the mark to kill them. This is where Jesus forecasted that fathers will turn in their children, and children will inform on their parents to be put to death for not taking the mark. It will be all or nothing; you give Antichrist you're all by this act, or you will be killed and in being killed will gain eternal life. As we get nearer to the Tribulation, parts of prophecy that we could not understand are becoming clear. It is getting so close now that if you do not know Jesus, you had better make sure you know Him, and if you are a believer, you haven't much time left to serve our Lord and Savior.

6

THE ABOMINATION OF DESOLATION

The abomination of desolation is referenced four times in the Scriptures, twice by the prophecy Daniel, two times by Jesus in the book of Matthew, once in the epistles and once in the Revelation. The first time it is mentioned in Daniel it is described as en end time event. The second time it is revealed as a key event and the number of days until the end of the world is given from the moment of its occurrence.

Jesus provides it as the main incident to look out for and warns the hearer to flee into the mountains upon witnessing or hearing of it. For immediately afterwards will be great tribulation such as the world has never known.

In 2 Thessalonians 2:4 a reference to the Antichrist in the Temple is made. It is the first place in Scripture where we are told specifically that the Antichrist directly sits in the Temple declaring that he is God. It states:

Let no one deceive you by any means; for that Day will not come unless the falling away comes first, and the man of sin[a] is revealed, the son of perdition,

who opposes and exalts himself above all that is called God or that is worshiped, so that he sits as God[in the temple of God, showing himself that he is God.

The book of Revelation does not mention the abomination of desolation directly but rather gives more details surrounded the episode. It also describes the events of the great tribulation that Jesus warned about.

After the Antichrist signs the peace treaty, economic prosperity follows the first three and a half years after the agreement. During this time, the Antichrist wins the favor among the masses because he leads the European Union into great prosperity, and all associated nations will grow financially.

As I stated in an earlier chapter, the four horsemen are unleashed and peace is taken from the Earth, but the Antichrist will use the wars and internal conflicts to his empire's advantage.

The Antichrist gains popularity through deceit. He has led Israel to believe he is their ally. Most likely, he will have already received his deadly head wound, possibly from an assassination attempt and he miraculously comes back to life (Rev. 13:3). The Antichrist's return from the dead—or near death—instantly increases his notoriety. The Antichrist allies himself with "the False Prophet" (Rev. 19:20), a member of the unholy trinity. A renowned religious leader able to perform miracles he campaigns for the Antichrist.

Now comes the moment he has been waiting for, he has raised the EU to its zenith of power. He leads the most powerful empire in the history of the world. Wealth and power are now his. At this time, he reveals his true self. It is now three and a half years after he made the agreement with Israel and it is in the middle of the seven year period.

He walks into the Jewish Temple, the third temple that is going to be rebuilt during the Tribulation and walks into the holy of holies and declares that he is God. He then places the abomination of desolation in the holy of holies, which might be a computerized clone of himself.

The Temple Rebuilt

During the first half of the Tribulation, the Jews rebuild the Temple of Solomon according to the exact dimensions described in I Kings, Chapter 6. With so many references to the abomination of desolation, we know the third temple will be rebuilt.

Currently, the Dome of the Rock, an Islamic Shrine which houses the foundation stone and a landmark built in 691 A.D., making it the oldest Islamic building in the world was constructed over the site of the second Jewish Temple destroyed in A.D. 70.

At present, in Israel a Fundamentalist Jewish movement exists that aims to rebuild the Temple. Within the Israeli government, the right-wing political party, the Temple Mount Faithful intends on constructing the Temple on the Dome of the Rock and also suggest building a new Temple on the site, in a place that will not interfere with existing buildings. They openly declare that their ultimate goal is the demolition of the al-Aqsa Mosque and the Dome of the Rock, and the reconstruction on their site of King Solomon's Temple. The Temple Mount is the holiest site in Jerusalem.

Jeremiah foretold the Temple's destruction by the Babylonians (26:6-12). Daniel predicted the Temple's desecration by the Syrian King Antichious Euphrates (Dan. 8:8-12). He also foretold Jerusalem's restoration and rebuilding by Herod and the Temple's destruction by the
Romans in A.D. 70 (Dan. 9:25). Hosea 3:4-5 foretells the long time the Jews remain without the symbols used for their worship, and without the Temple and how they will return to their God in the latter days.

For the children of Israel shall abide many days without king or prince, without sacrifice or sacred pillar, without ephod or teraphim.
Afterward shall the children of Israel's return, and seek the Lord their God, and David their king; and shall fear the Lord and his goodness in the latter days.

Daniel also foretells the desecration of a future third Temple, and the persecution of the Jews by the Antichrist (Dan. 9:25-26)

Destruction of the Dome of the Rock

Before this event, this prophecy will see fulfillment. The Jews will erect a new Temple which means that some future event will destroy the mosque and the Dome of the Rock that are on the site. This destruction will either happen from a natural disaster such as an earthquake or by war. Earthquakes have rumbled through the area in the past causing damage to the al-Aqsa mosque.

The Russian and Arab invasion predicted in Ezekiel may destroy the Dome of the Rock located on Mount Moriah. Bible scholars debate the timing of the battle. Some argue the war occurs prior to the Tribulation and others that this conflict takes place during the millennial reign of Christ. Either way we know some event will destroy the existing buildings, which will clear the area for the building of the third Temple. Most likely, the Temple will be rebuilt during the first half of the Tribulation.

The significance of this deed is how brazen the Antichrist will act by going into the holy of holies and declaring that he is God. In a previous, chapter I showed you the many parallels of Christ and the Antichrist and how the Antichrist tries to counterfeit Jesus. Just like his father Lucifer who wanted to be like God and was kicked out of heaven, now the son of Lucifer, the Antichrist walks into the holy of holies and declares that he is God on Earth. He also places something in the holy of holies, which may be his computerized clone that the False Prophet gave the breath of life. He gives it life only with God's permission. Notice from the passage the Beast is given life but not a soul. Revelation 13 :15 affirms:

And he was granted power to give breath to the image of the beast, that the image of the beast should both speak and cause as many as would not worship the image of the beast to be killed.

The Abomination of Desolation

Solomon's temple was a replica of the temple in heaven. We see the judgments coming from the heavenly temple in the

Revelation. Within Solomon's Temple, the "most holy place" (I Kings 6:16-36) housed the Ark of the Covenant. This sanctuary was the place God dwelt among the Israelites (Exodus 25). The Ark (made of shittim wood overlaid with gold) housed the two tablets of the Ten Commandments, Aaron's rod, and manna. Upon the Ark's mercy seat, the sprinkled blood of sacrificed animals atoned for all of Israel. It stood as a symbol of the blood of Jesus Christ, which would one day be shed and remit the sins of the world.

The Levitical priests performed the rituals and rites within the Temple. The priests abided by many details of dress, conduct, and worship. When the priests performed these rituals, God met with the children of Israel and sanctified the Temple by His glory (Ex. 29:43). All of these details and acts symbolized by animal sacrifice that blood was necessary for the remission of sin. These sacrifices foreshadowed the Messiah, who was to come and be the propitiation for sin. In the most holy place, God reaffirmed His promise to His people.

Without a Temple, no Orthodox Jewish person living today can practice his faith to the letter of the law. This explains the desire of some Jewish sects to rebuild the Temple, which is as great a part of Judaism as possessing the land, which God gave to the Israelites. The abominable act takes place inside the Temple. Daniel tells us about the

Antichrist's pompous words that he speaks at this time. Revelation 13:5 adds more details and tells us that God gives him this authority and allows him to make war with the saints and overcome them, and he gives him reign over every nation on Earth. Meanwhile, this desecration prompts the beginning of God's severe wrath and judgments on the Earth.

Satan Enters the Antichrist

After the Antichrist enters the most holy place and sits in the Temple and declares himself a god (II Thess. 2:4and terminates the worship and sacrifice, and commits sacrilegious acts, desecrating the Temple by setting the abominable thing in the Holy Place, his true character reveals itself.

We can assume that Satan himself enters the body of the Antichrist, just as he went into Judas Iscariot. The Antichrist will declare that he is God, will go into a most holy place and violate it, will have no regard for any human beings and will be capable of the vilest evil. He will hate all Christians and Jews especially and will also seek to destroy every one of faith.

Antichrist Wages War on Believers

At this time, he invades Jerusalem with an army (Joel 1:6, Dan. 11:31, 9:26), and lays siege to Israel, occupies its territory, and sets up a headquarters there and wages war against Christians and Jews, undertaking their annihilation (Dan. 11:33-35, 12:10, Rev. 6:10-11, Jer. 50:33, Joel 1:6, Matt. 24:9, Mark 13:9-13). Only a third of the Israelites will survive. Zechariah 13:8 declares:

And it shall come to pass in all the land, says the Lord; two thirds in it shall be cut off and die; but one third shall be left in it.

Concurrently, he and his federation of kings abolish all religion and their places of worship (Rev.17). At this time the Great Whore is judged by God. The Antichrist will not tolerate any religion other than the worship of, and devotion to, himself and his empire. Daniel 11:37 affirms that the Antichrist regards no man, and thus has no concernt for human life or suffering. The Antichrist launches a war against all believers in Jesus Christ, and many are martyred. God allows him to prevail and to accomplish his aims.

Christ Warns to Flee to Mountains

Christ solemnly warns the Jews in Judea at the time to flee to the mountains. He commands them to run and leave their jackets behind. He notes the additional suffering for pregnant and nursing mothers who must flee. In Matthew 24:21, Christ declares, " *For then there will be great Tribulation, such as has not been since the beginning of the world until this time, no, nor ever shall be.*" This is elaborated on in Revelation Chapter 11 and during which time the two witnesses appear on the Earth to testify and they perform miracles in the name of God.

God Protects The Woman From The Antichrist

In Revelation Chapter 12, we see the woman who represents Israel, who flees to the wilderness because she is pursued by the Antichrist. We are told in Revelation 12:15-17:

The Serpent spewed water out of his mouth like a flood after the woman, that he might cause her to be carried away by the flood.
But the Earth helped the woman, and the earth opened up its mouth and swallowed up the flood which the dragon had spewed out of its mouth.
And the dragon was enraged with the woman, and he went to make war with the rest of her offspring, who keep the commandments of God and have the testimony of Jesus Christ.

The Antichrist sends out his massive army to pursue the Jews and either an enormous sinkhole or an earthquake saves them from total annihilation.

Three And a half Years Left

The Book of Daniel and the Revelation prophecy give the number of days left until the end of the world from the day of the abomination of desolation, and it equals 3 and a half years.

The Antichrist now exalts himself above all, and speaks against the God of gods. He honors a strange god of fortresses by acknowledging and glorifying it and causing it to rule over many (Dan. 11:23, 36-39). This will be a weapon system, or computer infrastructure such as his mark. The Antichrist changes times and laws (Dan. 7:25). He has already made a statue or clone of himself, which the False Prophet causes to speak and that he has most likely placed in the holy of holies. Those who refuse to honor his image, he murders.

When the Antichrist establishes himself as s deity, the False Prophet will come out and perform miracles to campaign for the Antichrist. A sign of allegiance to the Beast is to take his mark. The False Prophet and the Antichrist wage war with those who do not take the Mark. He demands worship from the masses, and the crowds worship him (Rev. 13:8, 14-16). He prospers by accomplishing his aims.

Antichrist Conquers The World

The Antichrist's dreadful and terrible empire devours the world, and breaks it in pieces, with the speed of a cheetah. (Dan. 7:7, 8:24; Rev. 13:2).

The final world power is the equal of all the previous world powers combined, and its authority extends worldwide (Rev. 13:2). Revelation 13:7-8 confirms that *"authority was given him over every tribe, tongue and nation and all who dwell on the Earth will worship him."* The Antichrist initially gains the masses' admiration through his financial solutions and his ingenious peace proposals. He invades and conquers those nations that oppose him. Isaiah 10:14 records the power of the Antichrist's conquest in his own words. He declares:

My hand has found like a nest the riches of the people: and as one gathers eggs that are left, I have gathered all the Earth; and there was no one who moved his wing, nor opened his mouth, with even a peep.

This lines up with Daniel's description of a demonic, animal, metal beast, which rises to great power. Imagine that his army's power is so strong that people do not even fight back. It is almost inconceivable.

At that time the Antichrist's empire will

be the wealthiest on Earth. Technology will also be one of his weapons of war in addition to having the largest army in the world.

7

ANTICHRIST'S ARMY: 200 MILLION

One of the Revelation Plagues is the plague of the 200 million men army, which some expositors believer are a demonic army. Revelation 9:13-18 records:

Then the sixth angel sounded: And I heard a voice from the four horns of the golden altar which is before God,
Saying to the sixth angel who had the trumpet, "Release the four angels who are bound at the great river Euphrates."
So the four angels, who had been prepared for the hour and day and month and year, were released to kill a third of mankind.
Now the number of the army of the horsemen was two hundred million; I heard the number of them.
And thus I saw the horses in the vision: those who sat on them had breastplates of fiery red, hyacinth blue, and sulfur yellow; and the heads of the horses were like the heads of lions; and out of their mouths came fire, smoke, and brimstone.

By these three plagues a third of mankind was killed—by the fire and the smoke and the brimstone which came out of their mouths.

I do not hold that this is a demonic force but rather spiritual forces behind an actual army.

China's Army?

Years ago in Hal Lindsey's Book the Late Great Planet Earth he identified the army in Revelation 9: 15-19 as China's because China's population was so big their army numbered 200 million, and no other army in the world was that large. But, China makes no sense because we see China entering at the end at Armageddon in Revelation 16: 12 tells us:

Then the sixth angel poured out his bowl on the great river Euphrates, and its water was dried up, so that the way of the kings from the east might be prepared.

China also is also an illogical assumption that they should attack during the Tribulation because the Beast, the Final World Empire is going to be so powerful that it would be irrational for the Chinese to come out of nowhere and invade the world when the Antichrist has such a firm grip. What does make sense is for China along with Russia and the nations around the world to come against the Antichrist when he is in Jerusalem at the battle of Armageddon to defeat him. At this time he will need to be defeated. Remember he raises the EU to its pinnacle of power, and nations trade with his empire and there are good relations.

It is at midway through the Tribulation when the Antichrist steps into the holy of holies and declares himself as god that the Great Tribulation begins. He then institutes the Mark of the Beast, which he will have power to do because at that time, his empire will hold the world's reserve currency and will have the leading say in world institutions and will be the strongest economically and politically and militarily. The world will have to go along with his policies to benefit financially, remember all the nations are now connected economically.

Once the Great Tribulation begins, and he goes forth to conquer with extreme fury to conquer, he will gain control over countries in the Middle East. We know the Antichrist will control the Middle East region, and some of this area will be won during this conquest. Egypt will come into his hands during this time. When the Antichrist sets himself up in the holy of holy's as god and seeks to annihilate the Jews and all religion upon the face of the Earth, this might be the reason for the nations around the world to decide to come against him at the battle of Armageddon.

The EU Army

So who is the army in Revelation 9? It is the army of the beast. In the four horsemen of Revelation 6, we are shown that the four horsemen and the first horse is the prince on a white horse who goes forth to conquer. Revelation tells us their heads are like the heads of lions. The Beast has a mouth like a lion and Scripture tells us this in several places. Thus their heads are similar to the Antichrist's because they are an extension of him.

The colors' hyacinth blue and sulfa read are the colors of the EU military flag. There is also red in the breastplate and the Hebrew word for red is *pyrinos and it means shining like fire. brimstone sulfurous, Jacinth.* This army glistens because of its power.

The smoke, fire and brimstone with power and the mouth and tails sounds like artillery. When a gun shoots we see fire and smoke. What is worth noting that while the three elements are related, in the Bible they are referred to as three separate plagues, Rev. 9:18 *By these three plagues was a third of mankind killed-by the fire and the smoke and the brimstone which came out of their mouths.* This next verse sound like a belt-fed rifle or machine gun it reads, *"For their power is in their mouth and in their tails, for their tails are like serpents, having heads; and with them, they do harm.*

4 Horsemen Vs. 200 Million Army

In Revelation 9 we see that the Antichrist's army is 200 million men and is one of the plagues of God. The four angels accompany this militia and lend it their strength. One-third of the world's population is killed by this army. When we go back to the four horsemen of the Revelation, we see that war is also part of that campaign, but one fourth of the population is killed by the sword, famine and beasts of the Earth. In that battle nations rise against nation. This one is different and separate.

We do not know the exact reason for it, but we do know that Daniel describes the Beast as dreadful and terrible with great iron teeth and crushing power. This army goes forth and kills one third of the Earth's population. It could be the Antichrist's campaign for annihilation against those who do not take his mark and who are Christians, Jews or believe in one of the world's religions.

Population of EU Empire

The EU has 508 million citizens, during the Tribulation we know that some of the Middle East countries will be in its sphere of influence including Israel. We also do not know how much of Africa or India he might also invade. The EU population will be greater than it is today and can possibly produce armed forces of 200 million men.

EU Army Today

Today the EU has the world's largest standing army when you take the military of each of the member countries and add them together. While the EU does not officially have a military, the provision for one was laid out in the Lisbon treaty. EU leaders have already proposed giving the EU a full defense arm.

The horsemen of 200 million can be the number of heavenly horses that are released and do not correspond with the number of the army, but my hunch is that they do. Right now, the European union Military staff exists and when you add all of their forces together you come up with about 5 million men. This is personnel age 17-45, active, reserve and paramilitary. This shows us how big the EU Empire will become. During the time of Antichrist's conquest he will also enlist more than just age 17-45 volunteers, it will be mandatory to serve as under other dictators.

One can only imagine the fear, and dread caused as the EU military enters countries and towns and exterminates all who do not follow him.

8

10 DAYS OF TRIBULATION

The Antichrist's assault on Christianity and religion is a major facet of the Tribulation. It is also part of God's judgments on those who adhere to the beliefs of the many world religions, and the abolition of them. While the Antichrist will attack the adherents of all religion and their destroy their buildings and literature, his main targets are going to be Jews who have become Christians.

The treaty ushers in the final dispensation. The age of the Gentiles will come to a close and the focus will again be on Israel. Eternal life will be evidenced by not taking the Mark of the Beast. Revelation 20:4 tells us that many of these martyrs will be beheaded.

In the book of Revelation, Jesus walks among the lamp stands and speaks to the seven churches. Jesus addresses the church of Smyrna, which are the Tribulation

Christians, In His letter to the Church at Smyrna, He starts off by identifying Himself as the First and the Last who was dead but came to life. What is significant about Jesus stating that He is the First and the Last, is this how Jesus identifies Himself to John as He begins to reveal the Revelation Prophecy. They are now in the days of the fulfillment of the Revelation and the end of the age.

He tells them, *I know your works, tribulation and poverty (but you are rich.* This is because they have not taken the Mark of the Beast and cannot buy or sell and must live on faith. We cannot even imagine what it will be like to live under this kind of oppression. Tribulation Saints will not be able to buy any necessities. They are poor by the world's standards, but rich in Christ. Jesus then goes on to tell them in verse 9, *I know the blasphemy of those who say they are Jews and are not but are of the synagogue of Satan.* Both the church of Smyrna and Philadelphia do not receive any condemnation by Jesus. and in both letters Jesus makes reference to those who say that they are Jews but are not but are of the Synagogue of Satan. Jesus ends his message by stating in Rev. 2:10:

Do not fear any of those things you are about to suffer. Indeed, the devil is about to throw some of you into prison, that you may be tested, and you will have tribulation 10 days. Be faithful until death, and I will give you the crown of life.

Many have written about these ten days. Some have said it is ten years, others a period of time. I believe Jesus is talking about ten literal days. From the time after the arrest of the Tribulation Saints to their being thrown in prison and executed will be a total of ten days.

Under the US Judicial system, a person arrested for a death penalty crime can wait years on death row before execution. In dictatorships the executions or purges for those who are considered enemies of the State can go pretty quickly. It is not unlikely that the ten days of Revelation are literal ten days and are part of the protocol under the dictatorship. The Antichrist is not interested in imprisoning persons, but killing them.

What is interesting on the ten days of Revelation is that there is a parallel found in Daniel. The book of Daniel lines with the Revelation. Daniel is in Nebuchadnezzar's Babylonian Kingdom because of his intellect and good looks. He tells the eunuch set over him that he does not want to eat the food of the king because he does not want to defile himself. Daniel states in Daniel 1:12 *Please test your servants for ten days, and let them give us vegetables to eat and water to drink.* Jesus informs Smyrna that they will be tested, and they will have tribulation ten days. Daniel drank water and ate herbs and vegetables. Jesus is the living waters, and among the vegetables and herbs are the acrid herbs of the tribulation they are enduring and will now partake in the suffering of Jesus. The bitter herbs also represent Jesus's agony while on this Earth and the torment suffered by the Israelites while in bondage and servitude to the Egyptians.

Just as Daniel and his friends who lived on the meager sustenance of vegetables and herbs, the Tribulation Saints are thrown in prison and will only have a roof sheltering them from storm as any provision. The bread of life and Jesus's fountain of living waters will sustain them.

Daniel and his friends were tested ten days and at the end of the ten days their appearance was better and healthier than the men who ate the portion of the King's delicacies. During the Tribulation the kings fine foods come from taking the Mark of the Beast. Despite their tribulation they are in a spiritually healthy condition, better than those who take the Mark of the Beast and have this world's foods and luxuries. To God in heaven, their spiritual face is fatter and healthier than the persons who follow the Antichrist.

You will notice when you continue reading the book of Daniel, that the entire account is written for the Tribulation Saints. As the narrative of Daniel continues, we come to

Daniel Chapter 3, the worship of the golden image. Daniel tells us it is sixty cubits high and six cubits wide. We see a double six. Daniel does not worship the image. This mirrors Revelation 13 and the image of the Beast who everyone in the world is going to worship. The Antichrist's image is hooked up with the Mark of the Beast, and the Revelation tells us that those who worship his image also take the Mark.

Daniel and his friends get thrown into the fiery furnace and there is a fourth person in there with them, and we know this is Jesus. Daniel 11:32 states, *"that the people who know God shall be strong, and carry out great exploits"* Some will survive against all odds, while others will be killed. Others may start out carrying out great exploits and end up killed.

Again, we see Daniel is spared in the Lion's den while serving under Darius the Mede. His jealous governors made up a law that they knew Daniel by his faith in God would violate. The penalty was the lion's den. The lion's did not harm him. The lion is a symbol of the Babylonian kingdom and as I discussed earlier the lion is also a symbol of the Devil and the Antichrist. Revelation 13:2 describes the Beast as having a mouth like a lion. Just as Jesus is the pride lion from the tribe of Judah, Satan is the scavenger lion seeking whom he may devour.

Where do the Tribulation Saints end up but in the Antichrist's prison i.e. the lion's den. The Tribulation Saints when they go to prison will find themselves in the lion's den because the Antichrist is like his father Satan, a scavenger lion and his government possesses the mouth like a lion. Daniel 6:22 states:

My God send His angel and shut the lion's mouths, so that they have not hurt me, because I was found innocent before Him; and also O king, I have done no wrong before you.

Although the Tribulation Saints will find themselves in prison and will march to their deaths, essentially they emerge unscathed because Jesus tells us in Matthew 10:28 us not to fear those who can kill the body, but cannot kill the soul. As Daniel 6:26-27 affirms:

For He is the living God,
And steadfast forever:
His kingdom is the one which shall not be destroyed,
And His dominion shall endure to the end.

He delivers and rescues,
And He works signs and wonders
In heaven and on Earth,
Who has delivered Daniel from the power of the lions.

The lions are the Antichrist, his henchmen, the Devil and all of the powers of darkness that will be involved in this brutal murderous rampage of Christians. The picture of Jesus in the flaming furnace is a message for the Tribulation Christians .As face torture and death, they will not really be killed. The lion's den which is the prison they find themselves in, and the fiery furnace of their ten-day tribulation has no power over them. Notice what Jesus tells them in the beginning of his letter, He identifies himself as *He who was dead and came to life or who was dead and is alive or who died and came to life again.* What Jesus is telling them is though they are about to die, like Him, it will be meaningless because in Him, they will live after their death. alive in Christ and unharmed in spirit.

God will be with the Tribulation Saints in a very powerful way. Matthew 10:19-20 and Luke 12:11 tells the Tribulation Saints that when they are arrested and brought before rulers and authorities not to fear what they will say for the Holy Spirit will speak through them in that hour.

We see the martyred under the alter in Revelation 6:9-10 and we are told they are killed for the word of God and their testimony, and they are crying to God to avenge their deaths, in verse 11. they are given their white robes and told to wait longer as their brethren would be killed like they were.

During the Tribulation, you gain salvation by not taking the Mark of the Beast or becoming joined with him ., Jesus states in Revelation the devil is about to throw some of you in prison that you may be tested, and *you will have tribulation ten days*, and Daniel confirms, and it is written, *Please test your servants for ten days* and further down it says, *so he consented with them in this matter and tested them ten days*. These days are literal days from the time after the arrest to execution under the Antichrist's dictatorship.

So we have the picture of the horrible demonical person of the Antichrist and the climate he will create during the Tribulation. His army is so strong that the Bible tells us that he gathers the nations as a hen gathers its eggs, and as he invades the nations, they do not so much as let out a peep.

Revelation 12:11 states: *And they overcame him by the blood of the lamb and the word of their testimony and they loved not their lives until death.* The Tribulation Saints will have no life in the way that we life in any sense of the word. They will live on the run and their own family members will betray them. They will exist without the necessities of life and face torture and death. The Antichrist will hate Christians with a passion and he is going to seek to eliminate them from the ear

9

GOD'S JUDGEMENTS

The Antichrist's dictatorial reign is only part of God's judgments inflicted on the Earth's inhabitants during the Tribulation. As his empire rules cataclysmic earthquakes and radical changes in the solar system are going to boom. These all happen in addition to the war and pain inflicted by the Antichrist.

Countries will experience unprecedented famines, earthquakes, nations rising against nations in war and men murdering each other (Matt. 24:7).

7 Angels With Seven Trumpet Judgments

Along with the Antichrist's and man's violence and famines God unleashes the Trumpet and Bowl Judgments of Revelation. These come from the 7 Angels with the seven trumpets, and the seventh angel releases the seven bowl judgments.

Angel 1- Hail and fire burn up a third of trees and grass. (Rev.8:7).

Angel 2-A Volcano in the sea turns the sea to blood killing 1/3 of fish and ships. • The eruption essentially destroys a third of all sea life.

Angel 3-- A meteor falls like a torch in bodies of waters making them bitter and kills men who drink from them. This fallen star poisons a third of the Earth's waters (Rev. 8:10-11).

Angel 4-A third of the sun moon and stars darkens the day. Thus day and night reverse (Rev. 8:12).

Angel 5-Locusts, with stings like scorpions torment men for five months. This five-month plague of locusts stinging like scorpions leave men in agonizing pain and wishing for death (Rev. 13:21).

Angel 6-The army of 200 million kill one-third of mankind. (This we covered and is the Antichrist's army.)

Seven Angels With Bowl Judgments

Bowl 1 Loathsome sores form on those who have the Mark of the Beast.

Bowl 2 The sea becomes like blood, and all

sea creatures die.

Bowl 3 Rivers, seas, and lakes become as blood, and all sea and aquatic life disappear (Rev. 16:3-4).

Bowl 4 The sun becomes extremely hot, and produces a heat wave so severe it burns men with great fear and fire (Rev. 16:18).

Bowl 5 The throne of the Beast's kingdom darkens, and men gnaw in pain.

Bowl 6 This bowl is poured on the river Euphrates to prepare for Armageddon. Spirits like frogs from the mouth of the Beast, False Prophet and Dragon go out to kings on the Earth of the whole world to gather them to the battle of Armageddon.

Bowl 7 World-shattering earthquake causing landslides of such magnitude that mounts level. Resulting tsunamis bury all islands rains down on the Earth (Rev. 16:21).

We see from some of these plagues that while the Antichrist is used by God to judge the Earth, his kingdom also receives God's wrath. His government experiences a horrifying black out, and those who take his mark break out in grievous sores. This should not sound far-fetched as several types of body implants have been reported to cause major health problems such as with breast, dental and stent implants.

The thought of the cataclysmic natural disasters amidst famines, violence amidst the dictatorial reign of the Antichrist is unfathomable in the horror it will produce for the Earth's inhabitants.

Armageddon

After the Antichrist wreaks his havoc on the Earth, armies will go to fight against the European Union. Jeremiah 50:41 states: *"Behold, a people shall come from the North, and a great nation and many kings shall be raised up from the ends of the Earth."* In the Bible, North always refers to the area of the Soviet Union. *"A great nation"* may be the US. "At the noise of the taking of Babylon the Earth trembles, and the cry is heard among the nations" (Jeremiah 50:46).

God destroys political Babylon, i.e. the Antichrist's world empire. As Hitler was the spark for World War II, when he invaded and conquered nations in Europe; the Antichrist's swift and fast conquest will prompt powerful nations to wage war against him. Daniel 11:40 states that *"at the time of the end, the King of the South shall attack him: and the King of the North shall come against him like a whirlwind, with chariots, horsemen, and with many ships."*

Russia, the kings of the East, and a great nation from the coast of the Earth will strike and destroy the Antichrist's empire, possibly by a nuclear assault. Hearing of this, he goes out with extreme fury to destroy and annihilate many people. When armies invade his land, the Antichrist enters into the attacking countries and defeats them. He conquers Egypt and North Africa.

Hearing reports from the North and East, he goes forth with great fury to destroy. He ends up at a place prepared for him in Jerusalem (Daniel 11:42-45) and flees to his there because he will have control of Israel and portions of the Middle East.

Israel and the Middle East become part of Antichrist's conquered territory, giving him the exact borders of the Roman Empire at the time of Christ.

The invading armies confront him in Israel, and all the nation's troops join them at the battle of Armageddon (Rev. 16:16, 18; Ezek. 38; Jer. 4, 5, 50; Dan. 11:40-45). Jeremiah 4:6-7 tells us:

Set up the standard toward Zion: take refuge! Do not delay!: For I will bring disaster from the North, and great destruction. The lion has come up from his thicket, and the destroyer of the nations is on his way; he has gone forth from his place to make your land desolate; your cities will be laid waste without inhabitant.

The Antichrist's armies, the Soviet Union, the Eastern nations, and the US surround Jerusalem. The river Euphrates dries up, and prepares the way for the kings of the East, which are the Asian countries. God draws the world's armies to the place called, in the Hebrew tongue, Armageddon (Rev. 16:12-16).

At the Tribulation's end, Jesus Christ, shining bright as the sun, appears in the clouds with the saints and legions of angels (Rev. 19; Mark 13:26-27; Matt. 24:30). John Walvord records in his book *Daniel: The Key to Prophetic Revelation:* "The description of the time of the end confirms Daniel's revelation that it will be a period of trouble such as the world has never known, trouble of such character that it would result in the extermination of the human race if it were not cut short by the consummation, the second coming of Jesus Christ." The Antichrist and the world's armies attempt to make war against him.

The Antichrist's End

Revelation 19:19-21 records:

And I saw the beast, the kings of the earth, and their armies, gathered together to make war against Him who sat on the horse and against His army.

Then the beast was captured, and with him the False Prophet who worked signs in his presence, by which he deceived those who received the Mark of the Beast and those who worshiped his image. These two were cast alive into the lake of fire burning with brimstone.

And the rest were killed with the sword which proceeded from the mouth of Him who sat on the horse. And all the birds were filled with their flesh.

Christ casts the Beast and the False Prophet into the lake of fire, and slays the remainder of his forces by the sword of His word (Rev. 19:19-21). The Antichrist and the False Prophet will not experience the death of their physical bodies, and they will be cast directly into the lake of fire. They are both so vile and wicked in God's eyes that He sends them directly to hell. In the Bible, they are the first to be cast into the lake of fire. This is because they take the lead in evil. The rest of mankind who did not accept Jesus and was against Him in their lives follow behind. While the Antichrist is used by God to accomplish His wrath and purpose in the lives of the Tribulation martyrs during the Tribulation, at its end, he is condemned for judging Israel.

In several instances, you will read in the Bible that when God judged Israel and brought their enemies against them to accomplish his purpose, he then judged those who harmed Israel. The Antichrist comes on the scene because of the world's evil and while God allows him to wreak havoc in the world, he judges him. The Antichrist comes to his end in the lake of fire.

We know that alongside of our earth exists a spiritual world of principalities and powers that we do not see. Nor do we see the Holy Spirit or angels at work. However, when we pass from death to the afterlife, we see the spiritual world and some see this world as they are dying as if our physical bodies constrain us. At the second coming of Jesus there will be no constraint and the physical world will now see the spiritual.

The Day of the Lord

Jesus tells us that immediately after the Tribulation the world destructs. Matthew 24: 29-31 records:

Immediately after the tribulation of those days the sun will be darkened, and the moon will not give its light; the stars will fall from heaven, and the powers of the heavens will be shaken.

Then the sign of the Son of Man will appear in heaven, and then all the tribes of the earth will mourn, and they will see the Son of Man coming on the clouds of heaven with power and great glory.

And He will send His angels with a great sound of a trumpet, and they will gather together

His elect from the four winds, from one end of heaven to the other.

All the Old Testament prophets refers to the earth's destruction as *"The Day of the Lord."* Jeremiah 46:10 records it as *"a day of vengeance, a great slaughter, north of the river Euphrates."* The greatest earthquake in history levels and divides cities around the globe. Mountains cease to be, and islands sink under water. This is from the earthquake that causes major landslides that level mountains, and tsunamis that overflow and bury every island under water.

The sun darkens, stars fall from the sky, and the moon turns to blood. The sky looks like it is rolled up as a scroll. (Is. 2:12; Ezek. 30:3; Zech. 14:1-9; Zeph. 1; Joel 2:1-2, 10, 3:1, 15; Rev. 6:12, 16:9; Mark 13:24-25; Matt. 24:29).

The end of the sun's light and energy will cause the earth to go off its orbit. The stars falling from the sky will blow the earth to pieces.

The Millennium and God's Judgment Seat

The earth returns to its pre-flood state, and God judges the nations. Christ himself rules the earth for a thousand years, and binds Satan. At the millennium's end, God frees Satan, and he causes men to rebel against God. They surround the holy city, and God sends fire from heaven to devour them. God casts Satan into the lake of fire for eternity. At this time, the judgment seat of God takes place. Those whose names are not in the book of life; God casts into the lake of fire (Rev. 20:15).

God creates a brand new heaven and earth. The new Jerusalem descends from heaven, with streets of gold and walls of precious stones. The glory of God and the light of Christ illuminate the new heaven, and those who placed their faith in Jesus Christ live on for eternity (Rev. 21), while the evil and unbelieving suffer in hell.

10

Warning and Promise

The main message throughout this book is not just to educate you about the Antichrist, but also to tell you how to avoid him and the Tribulation altogether. The only way to circumvent the Tribulation is to know Jesus Christ as your personal Savior. If you are already a Christian, and you are reading this book for information on the Antichrist, you need to take warning because the time is near, If you are not living for Jesus Christ and not sold out to the Lord God of Israel and obeying the first command, you must do so today.

God's Messengers

God provides man the opportunity to seek Him during the Tribulation. "Two witnesses" prophesy for almost three and a half years. Men try to hurt them, and they smite the Earth with plagues that cause rain to stop, and water to turn into blood. The beast who ascends out of the bottomless pit makes war against them and kills them. The nations rejoice at their death. God raises them from the dead and lifts them into heaven (Rev. 11:3-13).

Tradition identifies these men as Moses and Elijah (Rev. 11:16) because God gave Elijah and Moses the ability to perform miracles and because they both appeared with Jesus on the mount of transfiguration (Matt.17:1-3). Some associate the two witnesses with Elijah and Elisha together as a team because of all the prophets, they performed powerful miracles, which included raising a person from the dead.

In addition, to the preaching of the two witnesses, during the Tribulation 144,000 witnesses, consisting of 12,000 from each of 12 tribes of Israel, preach the Gospel to the four corners of the Earth (Rev. 7:1-9, 14:1-7). During the Tribulation while God shakes the world with His power, He sends His messenger's. While a few will look to Him, the greater number of mankind curses God rather than turn to Him.

Despite the outpouring of God's anger and judgments, He still desires that men seek Him. Revelation 9:20-21 declares: *"after all of these plagues, man will not repent of his evil ways. Instead, he curses God."* This phrase repeats throughout the entire book of Revelation with each plague issued. This was the same reason that God brought judgment onto ancient Israel.

Those who become Christians during the Tribulation will most likely die because of the laws under the Antichrist and his pursuit of Christians or anyone of faith. While there is no way to escape the Tribulation once it has begun, there is route to avoid it altogether.

The Rapture

The Bible teaches us about Jesus Christ and forewarns the world about the horrific events that are yet to come. Those who have accepted Jesus Christ as their personal savior will not go through the Tribulation. God takes them out of the world in the Rapture just prior to the Earth's final seven years. II Thessalonians 4:14-18 tells us:

For if we believe that Jesus died and rose again, even so, God will bring with Him those who sleep in Jesus. For this, we say to you by the word of the Lord, that we who are alive and remain until the coming of the Lord will by no means precede those who are asleep.

For the Lord Himself will descend from heaven with a shout, with the voice of an archangel, and with the trumpet of God: and the dead in Christ will rise first:

Then we who are alive and remain shall be caught up together with them in the clouds, to meet the Lord in the air: and thus we shall always be with the Lord.

Therefore, comfort one another with these words.

In John's vision on the Isle of Patmos, he saw an innumerable multitude of people dressed in white robes, praising God. John asked who these people were. The angel answered him and said: *"These are the ones who come out of the great Tribulation, and washed their robes, and made them white in the blood of the Lamb"* (Rev. 7:9,13,14). Jesus tells the church at Philadelphia, He will keep them from the hour of trial that is coming upon the whole Earth.

In the Bible, there are instances of men of God who did not die but went straight up into heaven. These were Elijah and Enoch. Similarly the saints of God do not see death because just prior to the Tribulation they are Raptured out of the Earth and meet Christ in the clouds.

God ushered Lot and his family out of Sodom and Gomorrah before destroying the city. He commanded Noah to build the ark, rescuing his family from the flood. God brings those who have placed their faith in his Son out of the Great Tribulation. The Rapture occurs just prior to and after the sealing of the 144,000.

A major natural phenomenon may occur at the same time of the Rapture. Some may regard it as a rare occurrence of individuals disappearing into another dimension. Others may claim that aliens abducted the missing. Various experts will offer their explanations of how the disappearance of these people could have occurred. With strange events now occurring in nature, the Rapture will seem unremarkable to most of the world's inhabitants.

Jesus Returns As a Thief

The Bible mentions seven references to Jesus returning as a thief and seven is God's number of perfection. The Revelation mentions two of the seven. One of the verses in Revelation gives the same blessing we see in Luke saying blessed is he who watches or for those who the Lord Jesus finds watching.

The thief reference depicts Jesus's role in the Rapture. In the Rapture, Jesus comes when we are unaware, and he takes those of us who are his, and he takes us out of the world. It is as if we are literally stolen out of the Earth.

Jesus says in the Revelation to the church at Philadelphia, "I also will keep you from the hour of trial which shall come upon the whole world" We also have John talking to the elder and asking of the large multitude around the throne and the elder tells John, "these are they who have come out of the great tribulation and who have made their robes white."

Jesus gets very specific when He gives the

illustration of two women woman at the mill, and one is left standing still. He also states that there will be two men in the field, and one man is left in the field standing alone. This is not a reference to the end of the world return because on that day, there will be an earthquake that will divide cities across the globe, and 100-pound hail pounds and men are described as hiding in the cliffs of the rocks. Women will not calmly be grinding at the mill or a man standing in the field on that day.

The Three Wise Men

For those of you who do not feel that the Bible is clear about the Rapture consider this: The three wise men went directly to the birthplace of Jesus and greeted him with gifts of Frankincense and Myrrh. How did they know he was there? Micah 5:2 states Christ will come out of Bethlehem, Daniel 9: 25 gives a hint to the timing of the prophesied Messiah. Numbers 24:17 states, A star shall come out of Jacob. That is an ambiguous reference to most. The wise men pieced it all together and knew the star referred to a literal star and followed the star, which is Venus.

There are only so many days when Venus passes through and reaches maximum brilliance. The extreme crescent phase of Venus can be seen without the naked eye.

Herod inquired of the wise men what time the star appeared. This star stood directly over Jesus's manager. How did they know from so few references to come to the timing and birthplace of the baby Jesus? The Bible does not call them wise for nothing. Think of it, who would have thought that Jesus would have a star as a sign of his birth? An actual star shining against the sky over his manger. It is the same with the Rapture. The passages are there but not as obvious God expects us to study his word.

Jesus's Second Coming is Not the Rapture

When you read many of the passages minus, the ones in Revelation that are Rapture verses they sound like refer to Jesus's second coming, but His return at Armageddon is not like a thief. In Daniel and the Revelation God provides the number of days from the abomination of desolation so Jesus's coming at that time is not a big surprise. Because the Bible gives us the number of days, you know His coming is imminent.

At His second coming, Jesus appears in the clouds with armies as King of Kings. He is not coming as a thief at the second coming, He arrives as a King coming to battle. Jesus's arrival coincides with the cataclysmic end of the world so no one is going to be surprised. At Jesus's second coming there is not going to be a good deal of men left on the Earth. We know that ¼ of the world's population dies in war. We have the woes that affect a third of the population and finally, the great earthquake and 100-pound hail stones. Tsunamis' will be unleashed worldwide, huge landslides will occur from the leveling of the mountains, cities that will be divided and those who remain will be running for safety. This is not a setting for a thief. As Terry James wrote in his article a thief in the night, the Rapture begins the period of the day of the Lord.

The Rapture Will Appear as a Natural Disaster

Jesus is coming like a thief and will arrive when people are not expecting Him. He will take his own out of the Earth. The world will regard the event as if the people were stolen out of here. It is my feeling that the Rapture is going to occur alongside some bazaar natural disaster. When we see God's throne in Revelation 11:19 see thunder, lightening's great hail and an earthquake... Also around the throne and in our description of God and Jesus, we see fire and the light brighter than the son.

When Jesus said on the cross, it is finished, immediately there was an earthquake and the sun darkened. We also see in the Revelation when the seventh angel sounds it is done the earthquake occurs that divides cities across the globe. Around God and big events, we see His power and glory in things like thunder, lightening's, earthquakes and events in nature. When the Rapture occurs, there is something that will happen and cause those of us to appear to vaporize or disappear. Remember when this happens it might not be so obvious that Christians were removed because there are those going up who we would not think to have accepted Christ and there are those who we would think have accepted Christ, who will not go up.

Unexplainable Natural Disasters

When I think of a time in history when people have vanished, I think of the Bermuda Triangle with the disappearance of 50 ships and 20 airplanes in a 50-year period. Freaky was flight 19 on Dec 5, 1945. Flight 19, and a squadron of five U.S. Navy torpedo bombers, vanished into thin air during a routine training exercise in peacetime.

Before losing radio contact off the coast of southern Florida, Flight 19's flight leader was heard saying: "Everything looks strange, even the ocean," and "We are entering the white water. Nothing seems right." The aircraft and 14 crew members were never found, even more freaky, the search and rescue aircraft with 13 men sent to locate the missing planes disappeared too.

Talk about other strange natural disasters, The Tunguska event an enormously powerful explosion occurred in Russia on June 30, 1908. Over 1000 reports and papers later and scientists still are not in agreement about the cause and have speculated that it was made by the air burst of a large meteoroid or comet fragment (3–6 mi) above the Earth's surface.

Different studies have yielded varying estimates of the object's size, on the order of (330 ft.). It is the largest impact event on or near Earth in recorded history. The Tunguska explosion knocked down an estimated 80 million trees over an area covering (830 mi). It is estimated that the shock wave from the blast would have measured 5.0 on the Richter scale. This type of explosion was capable of destroying a large metropolitan area and was about 1,000 times more powerful than the atomic bomb dropped on Hiroshima.

Witnesses recorded seeing a bluish light, nearly as bright as the Sun moving across the sky. Along with a flash and a sound similar to artillery fire. The sounds were accompanied by a shock wave that knocked people off their feet and broke windows hundreds of miles away.. It will be the same with the Rapture. It will occur along with some kind of worldwide natural event. Those on the Earth will be left feeling like a thief snatched us away and assume we were vaporized by it. Similarly it will be like when the sinkhole swallowed the Florida man who literally disappeared and was never seen again. Scientists will come up with their theories as to what happened.

The Bible's Message of Hope

Although Bible prophecy presents frightening truths to the reader, its message is not entirely one of doom and gloom. Believers in Jesus Christ will not go through the Tribulation or have to live under the dictatorship of the Antichrist. If you know Jesus as your personal savior, God will take you out of the world in the Rapture just before it begins. God provides a way out. His way offers refuge and eternal life.

God's gift of eternal life with Christ is simple to obtain, but few will take it. All men are sinners. Sin is anything that we say or do that does not bring glory to God. God is righteous, and the slightest sin within us makes us unrighteous in His sight. There is nothing in and of ourselves that we can do to obtain the favor of God. Isaiah 64:6 states: *"And all our righteousness are like filthy rags."* God will not even accept one into heaven for his good works. Salvation is by faith alone. Ephesians 2:8-9 tells us: *"For by grace you have been saved through faith; and that not of yourselves: it is the gift of God: not of works lest anyone should boast."*

But Romans 10:13 promises, *"For whoever calls upon the name of the Lord shall be saved."* God promises eternal life to anyone who accepts Jesus Christ as his personal savior. John 5:24 states:

"Most assuredly, I say to you, He who hears My word, and believes in Him who sent Me, has everlasting life, and shall not come into judgment; but has passed from death into life."

If you want to be sure that you are saved and that heaven will be your home, and that Jesus will keep you too from the hour of trial that is coming on the whole Earth, and from the Antichrist pray this simple sinner's prayer and mean it with all of your heart and call upon the name of Jesus: "Oh God, be merciful to me as a sinner, I believe that Jesus died for my sins, and trust Jesus as my Lord and Savior. Thank you Lord Jesus for saving me." Romans 10:13 affirms. *"For "whoever calls on the name of the* LORD *shall be saved."* It is as simple as calling upon His name.

www.ingramcontent.com/pod-product-compliance
Lightning Source LLC
Chambersburg PA
CBHW070600170426
43201CB00012B/1886